ABOUT THE CURATOR:

Helen Calcutt is a poet, critic, and visiting lecturer in Creative Writing at Loughborough University. Her pamphlet, *Sudden Rainfall* was published in 2014. Her poetry and criticism has featured in publications such as Poetry Scotland, Southbank Poetry, and The Guardian, with award-winning essays in Boundless, and The Wales Arts Review. Helen's first collection *Unable Mother* was published by V.Press in September 2018.

In September 2017 Helen's brother Matthew took his own life. He was 40 years old.

ABOUT CALM:

The Campaign Against Living Miserably (**CALM**) is leading a movement against male suicide, the single biggest killer of men under the age of 45 in the UK. All receipts for sales of this book after bookshop discounts or Paypal transaction fees will be donated to CALM. You can read more about them and their campaign at https://www.thecalmzone.net/

Our deepest gratitude goes to all those who donated to our Eight Four crowdfunding campaign; this includes all the names listed below, as well as those who wished to remain anonymous.

Jinny Fisher

Clare Potter

Cherry Doyle

Jo Young

Antony Owen

Reama *

Abegail Morley

Sue Kingdon

Robin Hadley

Mel Pryor

Sue Sims

Stacey Witts

Nicky *

Hannah Swingler

Katie Hook

Adam Kirtland

Roxnne Gatrell

Ayla McCamphill-Rose

Ruth Stacey

Nadia Kingsley

James Hannah

John Mills

Liz Mills

Anna Metcalfe

Kerry Featherstone

Rishi Dastidar

Kate Oliver

Elizabeth Foody

Wayne Fox

Lou Sarabadzic

Olga Dermott-Bond

Aurelie Calcutt

Melanie Hanslip

Janet Jenkins

Janet Smith

Asim Khan

Jan Bartholomew

Roma Ante

Emma Purshouse

Chaucer Cameron

Leila Rasheed

Richard Archer

Anna Christina Price

Gram Davies

Casey Bailey

Theo Lloyd

Eighty Four:

Poems on Male Suicide, Vulnerability, Grief and Hope

VERVE
POETRY PRESS

BIRMINGHAM

PUBLISHED BY VERVE POETRY PRESS
Birmingham, West Midlands, UK
https://vervepoetrypress.com
mail@vervepoetrypress.com

FIRST PUBLISHED JAN 2019

Printed in the UK by TJ International

ISBN: 978-1-912565-13-9

*Dedicated to Matthew,
and his family, who have always
listened and loved.*

CONTENTS

Introduction by Helen Calcutt

Slipknot - *Jane Lovell*   15

Hide All the Knives - *Katrina Naomi*   16

Gaining Trust - *Romalyn Ante*   18

Impromptu - *MT Taylor*   19

That's Enough - *RM Francis*   20

The blood of Christ - *Brenda Read-Brown*   22

43rd Birthday - *Antony Owen*   23

Book of The Dead - *Nick Makoha*   24

Deciding - *Stephen Seabridge*   25

The decision room - *Abegail Morley*   26

Match Over - *Gary Carr*   28

Hollow Ponds - *Victoria Richards*   29

I should've said something - *Louisa Campbell*   31

Last Words - *Ian Patterson*   33

These boys - *Peter Raynard*   34

Red Road Flats - *Caroline Smith*   36

Multiple Choice - *Casey Bailey*   37

What About It? - *Liam McCormick*   39

my name is failure - *Charles Lauder Jr*   40

The Hunting Party - *Lewis Buxton*   41 my sister says - *Andrew McMillan*   42

Friends Who Decided to Leave in Their
Sequence of Leaving - *John Hawkhead*   43

One Bird - *Paul Howarth*   44

An incident with a train - *Paul Howarth*   46

sadness is a room - *Emily Harrison*   47

Mouth Organ - *Diana Cant*   49

Now my brother has died - *Helen Calcutt*   51

Wolf Blood - *Hannah Linden*   52

Boxes - *Richard Skinner*   53

An Evening With Lights - *Rosie Jackson*   54

Rise - *Bethany Rivers*   56

Body Balance - *Isabel Palmer*   54

A Boy Stands - *Belinda Rimmer*   59

Son - *Helen Kay*   60

Inscription - *claire e.potter*   61

Sitting Under a Pine Tree - *Zoe Piponides*   62

Rise - *Michelle Diaz*   63

face - *Alan Girling*   64

Time To Check In - *Salena Godden*   65

Just an aquaintance - *Alastair Hesp*   70

Eleven Men - *Joelle Taylor*   71

Lazarus - *Mario Petrucci*   73

Oiling Brakes - *Anthony Anaxagorou*   74

Seven Senryu in Memory of Brian Karr
Harter (1969-1987) - *Carrie Etter*   76

Rosemary - *Janet Smith*   77

Bath time memories - *Janet Jenkins*   79

An Improper Kindness - *Christina Thatcher*   80

The Ekphrasis of Self-annihilation - *Asim Khan*   82

A Single Atom in an Ion Trap - *Glyn Edwards*   83

What might live on the other side of
the moon - *Martin Hayes*   84

hold me warm blooded thing - *Shaun Hill*   86

In Which I Compose the Note but
Then Talk Myself into Living - *Gram Joel Davies*   88

Evening Prayer - *Abi Budgen*   89

A Dream - *David Calcutt*   90

Listen to this - *Stewart Carswell*   91

Notes & Acknowledgements

INTRODUCTION

A few weeks after my brother died, my daughter told me she could see his face in the moon. Days later, when she spied its silver disc in the window again she said that, actually, it wasn't just his face she could see. Everyone who had ever been sad was up there.

The moon changes, and so do all the people in its glow. And that was when I realised - we all suffer.

There's this idea that the personal blow of death, or a trauma, can't be relatable. And with society's insufferable ignorance to human vulnerability (especially male vulnerability) it's difficult to see how this could ever change. But I feel it can, if we stop the bullshit. If we accept the reality of the human condition – that it's a diverse, beautiful, troubled, elated, mish-mash of a being – and if we live by its natural demands, we can influence what is considered 'normal' behaviour. What currently stands as such has been working against us for generations, and ultimately, brought us to the mental health crisis we find ourselves in today.

There are other factors to this issue – foremost, lack of funds to mental health services. But change starts with the individual, and this is one of the reasons I created this book. I received little-to-no help from any authority or public service after my brother killed himself. The doctor signed me off for three weeks and I was offered pills. What does this do? This response, though an initial kindness, had no relevance whatsoever to the patterns of my complicated grief, and this signalled a twisted understanding of it, or worse, a normalised ignorance to my vulnerability, in all its ugliness and truth. It also exposed a desire to sweep the problem under the carpet. As was the police's response after my brother was found. Male dead, domestic tragedy. Tick the box. Move on.

It's my understanding that, at present, society is shaped to deny us our defining human quality: our complexity. To be human is to be vulnerable. It is also to be aggressive, quiet, commandeering, violent; it depends on the circumstance you find yourself in. But these are all naturally existing, powerful sides to us. For whatever reason, society encourages an over-simplified existence, thus generating accepted 'norms' to our behaviour. We live, we die. We weep, we laugh. We suffer, we feel joy. It would seem we're only ready to acknowledge and celebrate three of these six crucial human emotions. And the desire to live up to this warped standard of being has sadly become greater than the desire for truth.

Women cry, men do not. Men hit women, women don't hit men. Both examples of what we would consider a socially accepted norm, denies either party their natural complexity. Women do hit men, and though a violent and harmful act, it also highlights a particular type of vulnerability (perhaps a trauma too) that needs addressing. Men weep. It's probably one of the deepest, moving sounds I have ever heard. Denying this as a normal attribute to male behaviour, almost refuses them the bog-standard right to grieve, to shed a skin – to let it out.

Grief isn't just about death either. The effects of grief and trauma are very present in the body and mind of someone who has suffered divorce. The loss of a life we love, either from sudden house eviction to an extra-marital affair, can take 12 months at the very least, to overcome. We can even grieve, deeply and with absolutely profundity, the loss of our former selves in the wake of any personal travesty.

Not acknowledging the many possibilities, the many realities, to inner turmoil, is damaging. It represses and confuses us. Suicide rates are through the roof in the U.K. Male suicide stats are particularly devastating. 84 men kill themselves a week, my brother being one of them. The reasons as to why are complicated. And unknowable to us in many ways. But I will say that the pressures of a society largely unwilling to accept the anxiety and despair of a 'man's man' (holding down a job, a mortgage, child-care) will have had something to do with it.

The more we work to a fixed behavioural and emotional

'standard', the more we squash the natural intricacies of the broader human condition—not honouring or respecting who, and what we are. It's time we changed that. After putting out the call for submissions and contributions to this anthology, I can see I'm not alone in my thinking. The many poems I received, felt ready-made. Like they had been waiting at the bottom of a drawer for the perfect opportunity and place to speak. I'm glad those who submitted felt this was it. The poems published here, and the adjoining blog, have given this book the truth it was seeking, showcasing humanity in all its vulnerable beauty. From the baby in the bath who knows that daddy is gone, to the woman whose father haunts her like a wolf through the window, anthology Eighty-Four gathers an exquisite collection of voices, singing completely different hymns, but together creating a sincere and authentic piece of music. From well-known poets, to new voices, there's a glittering strength of character to this volume, because of the honesty from which its poems have been created, courageously and delicately embracing human complexity in all its forms.

I knew immediately the title would be 'Eighty-Four'. Inspired by the success of the #metoo anthology, I wanted to create something for a specific cause, that honoured and supported Project 84, by the charity CALM (campaign against living miserably) and drew attention to an issue in the only way I knew how: through poetry. But, for me, this number represents more than a devastating statistic. 84 men lost to suicide a week isn't a simple black and white problem. And the problem itself, isn't a symptom of any single cause. It's part of a wider dilemma, acutely connected to our almost pathological denial of human fragility (connected perhaps, to our fear of immortality and death). If you're reading this, you may not feel an immediate emotional connection to male suicide. But you can understand the prevalence and seriousness this number holds. You might also start to understand what it means for us as a society, and share in asking the crucial question: how shamefully oppressive have we allowed the world in which we live, to become?

Together, with the creative minds at Verve Poetry Press,

CALM, and my wonderful father and co-editor, we have created a book that, in opening its doors to the devastating theme of male suicide, has inspired a river of additional sub-themes and contexts: all relevant and connected to the central theme. At one stage, I considered grouping the poems under different chapters. But with time, I saw this wasn't necessary. Anthology Eighty-Four has taken on its own life and shape, with each new phase of reading, though distinct, somehow aligned and in harmony with the one before it. There are poems here that sing to each other. Words and images that relate, yet with their altered backdrops, offering new perspectives. There are clear changes in voice and tone: the angry man, to the angry bereaved. This kind of opposition (or 'balance' as I like to call it) gives this anthology the emotional range it deserves, and is an authentic reflection of the overwhelmingly diverse, and sustained effects of suicide. Each poem conducts its own careful truth, told with searing conviction. Light and shade.

This book is for every single person who has ever felt silenced. For anyone who feels uncomfortable talking about trauma or grief, to those currently suffering from grief-by-suicide, or who want to learn more about mental health issues. Let this be your touch-stone. Not only does it prove how powerful poetry can be in bringing our injured worlds into view, it also exposes a new, hopeful reality. Saying to you -start talking, and keep going. Live through, and voice your vulnerability. Speak and live your humanity.

This book is also for Matthew. The older brother who was always giving. The first one to call me and tell me everything was going to be okay when I was pregnant. Whose laughter filled the room, and infected every single person in it. Who was honest about not liking poetry. Who listened, and reserved judgement. Who was open and giving to every other human flaw, right to the end. Just look how this generosity has inspired others, and lived on.

Helen Calcutt (Dec 2018)

Eighty Four

Slipknot
Jane Lovell

This starts with a white cat
caught like a mink in the scrub,
the skin of its hip slippered off by wire.
We set it free, you and I, that spitting fury,
watched it rocket from the ivy
through the fence and away,
tracked it jinking in that lop-sided way
across the frost-pocked hill.

That deep, embedded cord
I fix into another poem,
coil into a neat circle, press it shut
but cannot erase, ten years on,
the folding of the paper, dust motes
flying your name in the morning brightness,
words read out by a stranger,
that quiet 'oh' and nothing more

or you, like that,
hanging like a manikin,
eyes fixed on that swarm of black bees
percolating through the trees.

Hide All the Knives
Katrina Naomi

That's what I remember most –
the nurse from the NHS helpline
his telling me to *hide all the knives.*

Until then, I'd not understood
or refused to understand
your laying in bed all day, all night,
face to the wall. Suicide –
you couldn't mean it,
could you? You who was always laughing –
the life and soul.

All those blades: the bread knife,
with its serration, the two vegetable knives,
the posh knife from foodie friends,
which I never used, our penknives for outdoors,
I wrapped them in my cardies
to keep them soft.

You told me:
I'm worthless
I want to kill myself
I'm a terrible person
I deserve to die.

You stopped washing, your quiff
flopped, grew a different kind of grease.
You wouldn't talk.

I didn't know you anymore,
though I tried to tell myself
I loved you.

I didn't feel right, naked in bed next to you/not you,
wished I had pyjamas,
though the person who wasn't you looked
nowhere but at the wall, eyes stagnant.

The emergency pills knocked you out,
the others slowly turned your eyes
blue-green again – as if they'd been photoshopped.

You still couldn't talk to me
but spoke to a kind woman
in a room with pastel walls and Monets.

Weeks later, I found you,
smiling, through a room thick with hairspray,
as you rummaged in the wardrobe
for your red and orange Hawaiian shirt.

Gaining Trust
Romalyn Ante

But there are still voices that tell her to lick
the shadows dashing across the floor.
There are bones beneath the bed, their metallic

grate. And the heart is a fist that twists the door-
knob, wanting to get out of the pitch-black ribcage.
There are dead people in hospital gowns and more

trail behind her every day. There are bunches of sage
her mother burns but the kid with an algae wristband
still curls at her feet. There is the sharp edge; the rage

of red clouds; a gun at her temple held by a hand
that is hers, but not.   At school, she weeps
when the end of the hall peels off into a farmland

or into a train platform. A girl in uniform leaps
out of her body and splatters on the rail track.
How did you convince her to keep

her palms pressed on your back
while you stand firm at the yellow line?
Here comes the supplication of the tracks.

Impromptu
MT Taylor

My father's brother would come to stay
at the end of the year.
He would leave the wife at home with the kids

- said something to do with the cost of the flights
but I heard his wife had no time for the North
and his Northernness.

He would sit at the piano which belonged
to his father - still with us then
and play for himself.

We would leave him to his piece
filling our home with winter light
grateful for such unexpected grace.

One Sunday morning,
he threw himself from the roof
of a city centre car park
near his house in London.

On the day of the funeral
I asked his wife why
there was no piano in their home.

She said there was no room.
I understood at once
that he had never really lived there.

That's Enough
RM Francis

With your massive car and your tiny wife and chickpea mousse that keeps you so humussed and Will Self novels you pretend you've read at brunches with the other dads who hate you too, and you're right, they do all think your beard is too thick for a man your age and it's not okay to wear scarves indoors. You should be scared of us. You should be fucking scared of us, boy.

You call it a man cave but you've always been useless at being a man and those tools and that dartboard and the whittling starter-kit you got for Father's Day are all still vacuum packed in plastic, like the 4x4 discussion you tried to have with that bloke in the Cross Keys. It's a shed, mate, and you only use it to listen to your Arcade Fire CDs, you really wanted your youngest to like them but he's too busy with live action role play games like those shits from Stranger Things, and sometimes you rub sawdust and WD40 into your jeans, don't you? When your tiny wife comes calling for her allowance, don't you? You should be scared of us. You should be so fucking scared of us, kid.

Then there was the time you all went to the protest picnic, your tiny wife made falafel from a recipe in the Huffington Post and the Hassan's giggled a bit, you made it alright though, didn't you? You know, when you laughed with Syed about hipster appropriation, and you'd made cute signs for your seven year old and even she saw the irony in your irony but kept her head as you smiled with high eyebrows when the man from the Central News asked for her opinion on American immigration policy. You. Should. Be. Fucking. Scared. Fella.

Then it's pack up the massive car and back to the massive bed, too wide to cuddle, and you tweet like you've made your life and you stare at the ceiling and you read the testimonials to *My Idea of Fun* again and think about starting it but it's late and it's Sunday and they've all been a bit much today, what with Sophie's cookies, that's Judd's wife, she's lovely, Judd, lucky fucker, even his name is better, Judd. There's no room for you anymore, mate, not with all those syllables. You stare at the ceiling and you think about shaking one off. Your tiny wife is done in, you can hear her stupid fucking breathing, and you stare and you should be scared.

When you ran away. When you thought about running away, you took the second car, the hybrid, the young wench from the Greens told you about climate change and you thought that'll make a decent selfie and its one way in to that weird dad-sex-fantasy you'd been having. You took the hybrid and drove as far as Birmingham and nursed a pint and a scotch egg and the sun was out and you gulped back a whiskey and went home, and you should be scared, mate, you really should be scared.

Two weeks ago the landlord told your wife to shut her legs and they all laughed. You thought folding your arms was enough, and you should be scared. Two days ago you crossed the road 'cause the lads by the shops wore tracksuits and looked swarthy, and you should be scared. And today your shaving off the beard and you're going to start doing push-ups. You used to be a pretty good runner so think about that, and then you watch an old Werner Herzog film and then you buy some new shades but your tiny wife has news for you, boy.

In your massive car in your massive garage you sit for a few minutes longer than you need, and you breathe, and you look at the length of the side panels through the mirror and the tube it would need to run from exhaust to window and you really think ... this time you really think.

And I told you to be scared of us, didn't I?

The blood of Christ
Brenda Read-Brown

"If I'm going to die, then you're going..."
but he didn't finish the sentence,
not that one,
nor the other one, the one for life,
alone, kids stolen, house stolen,
wife stolen. He escaped
punishment for the crimes
committed against him,
set himself free
in the car that was all he had left,
two daughters and a son
in the back seat.

And did he, in those last moments
between the splash of impact
and the submission
to submersion,
moments that must have been hours
of dark and cold and crying,
did he, when the crying stopped,
and his mouth filled with lake water,
did he taste it as communion wine,
and forgive them?

43rd Birthday
Antony Owen

Suicide is the single biggest killer of men aged under 45 in the UK. In 2015, 75%
of all UK suicides were male. - CalmZone

Unearthing you is a disturbed treasure,
that last glass of red grainy as a Truprint sunset
the immaculate house and your note of broken maps to why.

To say your name is to bring you home in a wooden birdhouse.
Each time I see our Mother blow you out in Rothmans
she remembers your incense, the birth and still deaths.

To say your name is to admit you go to God grey and cold.
Each time I see our Father he is a cradle of bone
there are holes instead of eyes, tomb dark.

Unearthing you is the colour of Facebook blues and reds,
ninety-four comments that say nothing and everything,
sixty-three emoticons weep at a coffin of pixels.

Book of The Dead
Nick Makoha

To you the already dead, to those dying
in their sleep, to those flooded by a wet
season that did not wait for next year's crop.

To the weeping, the wounded. To those hiding
in the fever of a night waist deep in mud.
To those standing in line for the body of Christ.

To the smoke, the only thing that rises
without interrogation. To the thirst left
in the mouths of men, quenched by the glass
of a woman, the glass of another country,
the glass that is not a glass but a truck filled
with bodies hemmed together by barbed wire.

A truck that yesterday was filled with toxic barrels,
and before that money, and before that money.
To you who chew with your mouths open
as I become a desert and a war zone.

To those empty spaces that exist when a man's
words become familiar ghosts. To those who spoke
of rebellion before the moon crawled on to their backs,
and now their bodies itch with maggots in a ditch.

To the palm of the immortals who raised the river from its bed
and had its waters stare a man in the eye. To the never-ending
silence that knew us before we were human. To those that thirst
and hold their hands like brackets waiting for thunder,
searching for the shape a body makes when in prayer.

Deciding
Stephen Seabridge

There comes a point when it settles in,
an old, familiar blackness, old, familiar dark
that is more than a lack of light,

but you cannot imagine death yet,
you know that there are few ways of doing it,
inflicting it upon yourself, without more pain,

without more of the numb, hollow band
in that space that must exist behind the chest,
that space undetected by science,

so you lie there, in bed, or on the floor
pressed hard to the cold tiles, or the carpet
a hot field of hair digging into your cheek,

you lie there, still as the sun streams in,
still as the rain, still as a knife suspended
between the far points of everywhere.

The decision room
Abegail Morley

There's a deep frost, salt-crisp, and if I lick it
I'll taste the very end of the night before,
when you shut your front door, went upstairs
to where there was only just enough air left for
one breath and only just enough time to decide.

And somewhere in that pitch-dark space
where your breath finished in your lungs
you shaped the beginning of your end.

It is your pre-jump. Your vault. You step from
your body, two foot from where my bed is now,
without the slightest hope of a second chance
leave it behind like a moon blighted by clouds.

You tugged open every drawer and they stuttered
on rough wooden runners, hung lopsided and you
pulled sweater after sweater, shirt after shirt, until
deciding what to die in became impossible.

It is 5am when the police come. Ice-white fields
aren't yet disturbed, nothing creaks.
The doorbell's shrill is a terrible wrong.

I'm thinking about the coldness of morgues
and have so many clothes to keep me warm
a shoddy dropped mess of them, a pulled out,
thrown down, skinless you.

*Most times I remember the whole of you, but
sometimes I can't help remembering how far you fell.*

Match Over
Gary Carr

Every bat has a dust heart
drawn on its surface
by the end of a match.
We all have our rituals
to wipe it clean, ready
for our next opponent.
Most players are a chaos of kit –
bat, spray, covers, sponge –
but today one sits quietly,
equipment squared
to table sides, the way
you used to. Two squirts
per side, you would wipe
each, in careful strokes,
away from your body.

I heard that you had tidied
and everything was square
when they found you. Even
your incisions were precise.
Your heart, dust. Loss wiped,
finally, away from your body.

Hollow Ponds
Victoria Richards

The lonely men stand by the lake. They watch moorhens bob
    and weave,
poke plastic, a pair of swans pissed off with each other –

pissed off by the way they're always used as a symbol of perfect,
    unstinting love,
when they can't fucking *stand* each other. Because monogamy is
    difficult for anyone,

let alone those who swim in circles round and round the same,
    wet pond.
The lonely men know this. They roll and swell with their plastic bags.

What are they waiting for? To fuck to be fucked to suck to be sucked.
    To lose themselves
in that frantic rutting, the scratch of rough bark –

to drown out their loneliness, which is never drowned out for long.
They're back again one day, three days, five hundred days later

wearing the same nervous disappointment, boots shifting over
    leaves, rollercoaster eyes.
While a heron sits steadfast on a post warning swimmers

not to even *think* about trying to wash their sins away in this
    hollow lake –
like anyone would choose to go for a dip on the first freezing
    morning of November.

One of the lonely men steps forward. Scraps of toilet paper kiss
        the trees,
a string of condoms hangs like fairy lights.

It is his first time. Should he bite deep into rough soil, push it
        throat-wards,
a dirt clod embalming?

It tastes the way his teeth taste the morning after a bottle of wine
        – two bottles.
Some ill-advised whisky.

A goose sidles by. Unmistakeable: the slow waddling,
        the casual whistle
of tail feathers tucked beneath. Soft down, hiding its secrets.

The lonely men with plastic bags hide their secrets beneath
        their webbed feet.
Wait for the glass-smooth surface of the water to break. To ripple.

I should've said something
Louisa Campbell

when the penny dropped
and kept on dropping
down in darkness.
I couldn't hear it hit the bottom.

I should've said something
when I walked past the doctor's,
walked back,
walked on.

I should've said something
when I couldn't see good
any more and couldn't tell
if it was there.
Is it still there?

I should've said something
when I found myself Googling,
how far must you fall?
how tie a noose?
how long does it take to drown?

I should've said something
when I realised I knew
which motorway bridges
had fences for rails;
which were still open.

I should've said something
when I drove to the top
of the concrete car park,
climbed on the wall,
took off my red scarf,
let it go, let it all go,
watched it ebb quietly down
to the empty street below.

I should've said something
when I made the decision
and that gave me peace, as if
the ogre that rode on my back
with his arms round my throat
and his legs round my waist
had tumbled off,
thudding.

I sh

Last Words
Ian Patterson

October's sun was a cold hard spotlight,
glaring through railings, houses,
warehouses, trees.

This half empty train was your private
commute. As we pulled out of the station,
you looked up at me from the front

of a discarded newspaper, as someone
stood up, and smoothed their coat. At
the next town, office workers

in dark blue and black, stood waiting,
then dragged their long shadows up to
the train. Outside the station,

people walked, buses and taxis idled,
two billboards stood waiting, each
one holding your name.

These boys
Peter Raynard

JONNY – we used to drive him mad playing with his locks
in year 8 computer science, began coding in juniors, quiet
like but you knew when he was in any room – TED - straight
arms, wrists handled behind his back, a lean to of *'come, and
have a go'* – laid out on the table like a victim – his own worst
enemy doesn't even cover the body - CHARLIE - had a skate-
board stuck to his feet – life was a grinding rail – never said
why he was in care - why he couldn't stay in one place –
everyone has some kind of darkness but he had nothing but –
MICKY – grew so tall must have been raised in a greenhouse,
could drop a three-point basket sitting down, boy could he
fly, can still feel the breeze of him, hear it too, always
chatting some kind of shit, usually about some girl – BEN –
got the weed off his big brother - bottom of the frosted fields
lunchtime, cold air hiding our smoke – totally licked for
session 5, still don't know how we got away with it – i
guess he didn't – JACOB – turned right up high on
repeat, probably addicted to teletubbies in a
previous life, wanted everything again/again – first week of
university must be a mad thing, more of the more,
knocking down your door – in English he'd sometimes
say *'who gives a fuck what the dead think'* – must have got
curious though, because he fucking knows now – no-one
wants to know the definition of an epidemic - the put upon
of people – everyone knows someone – everyone flicks through
the channels of their supersized packages unable to watch the
morphine dance – teachers count the A graders – count the
graduates – count their dwindled coffers – they count the
absences of these boys – these boys left hanging over

their homework – these boys hiding in the woods (always the woods) – these boys given to impetuous - these boys who now sit round that table upstairs their lips sewn together by the expectation of masculinity signing what the fuck did you expect?

Red Road Flats
Caroline Smith

When the Presenting Officer heard of
their suicides following the ruling
it was as if he'd woken up
and found himself
a trespasser in his own garden.
He read back through the files,
began to doubt his own certainty.
What he had dismissed as paranoid, he
now saw from within their world as real,
not benign, not to be trusted,
just as an early morning frost brings out
a previously invisible conspiracy of
white cobwebs connecting the grasses.

Multiple Choice
Casey Bailey

Find a new place to hang this noose.
Stop killing those who already killed themselves
like they haven't suffered enough already,
carried enough already,
died enough already.

To label somebody a coward
when they are no longer here
to represent themselves,
has to be the worst cocktail
of cowardice and hypocrisy
I have tasted.

Maybe he did it because he
had lost all hope in this life.
Maybe she did it because her only hope
was that another life would follow.
I always thought the most difficult
multiple choice questions
are the ones where you feel like all
of the answers could be right.

Gravity is pulling us all down
just because bricks fall faster
than feathers,
doesn't mean they're weaker,
they just carry more weight.

A man who looked young
but aged, with a face
like distressed furniture,
told me that the greatest
misconception about suicidal people,
is the thought that they want to die.
Nobody desires death,
the issue is, that not everybody
wants to live, either.

The most difficult multiple choice questions
are not the ones where you feel like all
of the answers could be right.
The most difficult multiple choice questions
are the ones where you feel like none
of the answers can be right,
but you must choose one anyway.

What About It?
Liam McCormick

He is buying women's things for his missus, y'know:
£1 bar of chocolate, weird crisps he's never heard of
And a pack of sanitary pads, the big ones, big 8 hour job.
Needs to make the money s tr etc h.
'Oh and 30 grams of amber leaf.'
The cashier notices and with a matey wink quips –
'These are getting bloody expensive.'
He retorts, *'Well what about the male suicide rate?'*

When he gets home she says he's bought her fucking nappies.
She'll just go herself next time, godsake.

Nailed it.

my name is failure
Charles Lauder Jr

I am an ice skater
arm swinging   heart racing
etching the surface
in sharp lithe swipes.

I let the sting sing
how deep
the blade has cut
how quickly it shows

I'm never brave enough
to run the whole length
from my little hole
to a place of numbness.

Just enough to punish
for falling   not once
not twice   but each time
in front of everyone.

The Hunting Party
Lewis Buxton

There is a hunting party
after us and we are just beaked
and feathered boys listening
to the beaters crashing
through undergrowth,
our plumage heavy with rain.

We are easily startled, such sensitive
creatures, we have friends
and fathers in that hunting party,
that want us dead or different.

Remember, as the mouths of shotguns
scatter-pattern warning shots, our bodies
are worth more than their meat.
Dogs are barking, we can hear
their lolling tongues: words are teeth
and all our feelings are flesh.

When they shoot us from the sky
and send the dogs to collect
our bodies, they will barely notice
how buckshot ruined our feathers.

When they pluck the courage out of us,
butcher what is left for dinner,
only then will they be proud
of how soft we were, how tender.

my sister says
Andrew McMillan

we tell the children its a glass of water
that's always almost full to the lip
any extra overwhelms it

there is a bucket under the bathroom light
to catch the dripping rain   trouble
seeps through your skin   nightly   the glass fills

until it topples and we try to gather
up the spreading water in our hands

Friends Who Decided to Leave in Their Sequence of Leaving

John Hawkhead

The first shot himself on an empty beach,
his final echoes ricocheting between
a hard land and the relentless sea.

The second took a length of rope
and set himself adrift in an empty room
silent as his unbeating heart.

Then two more; brothers riding
the black dragon of addiction
into the pit of its eyeless maw.

One more took a tortured leap
from clifftop into the void,
the cold salvation of nothing.

And finally the lone motorcyclist
who could have made a mistake
as he crossed the white line

between here and never, a mistake
on a stretch of the straightest road
a broken man could follow.

I.M: JH, KM, FT & NT, DT, AT

One Bird
Paul Howarth

Unbegin:

Just there. Look. A blacker against the black.

Flocks

and scatters a one bird murmuration. A
squaller against the squall. Carries the
weight

of his own empty hands. Falters and stoops.
    Unveins an ellipsis, all across the graveyard
    path.

            Unvoice
                              Unword
                Undefine

                      Unman
            Unman
                                    Unman

                Unbear
                              Unweigh
            Unfold

Falls and unfalls. Anchors to the church porch.
Screams a submission to wind and ascent.

Leaving behind the massing storm
and a shelter. A sheltered but

empty

space. A rage, a final rage of grace.

:unend.

An incident with a train
Paul Howarth

The local news will describe this as an incident with a train,
because no-one wants to read what really happens when a
solitary human being collides with that velocity of despair.
Official statements will be performed as preformed - with
intent to still. Stress the fullness of investigation, the
minimised disruption to your commute. There will

be no dwelling on the life or the death of it. The
convulsing mother, degraded to salt. The junior police
officer fighting back puke, weighing alternative career
options against the chances of promotion and a desk.

The trembling, day-glo railway worker who
yells at the edging crows, *fuck off, fuck OFF.*
Throwing stones to ward them from the spoils:

it's hard, even at the best of times,

to look solemn in a hi-vis vest. It's hard to hold together.

sadness is a room
Emily Harrison

sadness is a room –
you moan from
its bed on bleached
floors – white sheets.
The nurses are rushed so we ask;
can you wash him please?
As if they have lapsed, forgotten,
he can no longer speak.

Be there in five, she says –
we move the L you slide yourself into
like a hot curled child now
awaiting arrival on
plastic chairs where grief is
stalling for suture.

It takes her ten, you cry
throaty for the duration gargling
dry. We consider a moment
that once would've been clear –
can we soothe him?

And it's unimaginable –
rootless as the breeze
blowing across medicinal landscape, lost,
that we are unsure of the procedures –
how to gift him water.

Eventually she comes –
you might be better leaving whilst
we nod toward each other,
not the nurse, but whisper
be gentle to her as we go
to waiting rooms of would-be funeral mourners –
solemn miles to mortuaries, no,

we have arrived at purgatory instead.

Mouth Organ
Diana Cant

This is the morning she sits on the table,
drumming a rhythm with her heels
on the cupboard below.

I long to be elsewhere

Unremarkable brown hair strewn across her eyes,
pink socks, floral leggings and a jumper
with a picture of a kitten.

elsewhere in my mind and in my body

She glares disdainfully
as she eyes the toys on the shelf
and reaches for none.

to turn my back on memory and desire

This is the morning she begins
to say something
of the way her life has been.
Her saying has no rhythm,
no easy coherence. Instead,
only fragments of fear.

to be suspended in a space without meaning

What she knows, she knows without words;
she is blind-walking her way
through the alley-ways of pain,
towards a searing truth
made more bearable
for being wordless;
made more bearable
by the absence of the nailing words of knowing.

disconnected

Her drumming stops,
as she reaches for a small mouth organ
lying on the shelf,
and begins to play
the keening song
of what might have been,
but never was.

sadness, such sadness streams from my lips

Now my brother has died
Helen Calcutt

the flowers have opened. Somehow the sound of a river
is moving in my head.
Somehow the startled flowers.
Or is it blood? Heart,
the ephemeral mouth
opening and closing. How dare it grant me
this steady life. The strength of it.
I want a stillness, still I
go on, like the soul of a river, living loud with
other rivers, longing for murdered flowers
and for the sudden resurrection of a hanging
clock.
How dare this life
make me want the things I'd die to love,
but river-bound, never could.

Wolf Blood
Hannah Linden

I said to Death, *here is my window*. Light from my father plays
with the scenery and all the shadows breathe with his breath.

Death said, how can you bear the strength of the sun, child?
Come with me into night and sing with the moon and her
reflections –- midday sun, with its lack of apology, will not
spare you. Take your father's shadows and wrap them round
your shoulders. Howl at the moon and let your tears fall. Here
you will not age and forget. Here your father is always young
like he was when he loved Death more than he loved his
children, his moon, the sun. *Be with us, child.*

And my wolf blood rose in me with its cry of glory and
desolation. How I wanted death and my father. How I wanted
to run the moon down — my belly ached with the hunger. My
children could smell my blood-lust, smell the wolf of my hide.
And I was afraid. My son took my hand and kissed my fingers.
My daughter slapped her teenage longing in my lap.

*Open the window, mother. Take the cape from the box under your bed
and come out into the sun and play.*

Boxes
Richard Skinner

You always hated my boxes.
The black belt box with its gold lettering;
the Art Nouveau tin of mints from Montreaux;
the red marbled box that held a bottle of wine.

You never understood why I
kept them in my wardrobe. The top cupboard
in the kitchen is always empty. 'Why?' you asked.

Then your mother died and you snapped like elastic.
Your breath turned sour and you drank wine
all of the day and all of the night.

Our grief composes itself in the whole space
of the upper body and comparts itself
into packets, boxes
that only then can I throw away.

An Evening With Lights
Rosie Jackson

for Elaine Alpert, who lost her 16-year old son Rand to suicide in May 2004. She now runs programmes to support other mothers bereaved this way.

Imagine a mother. Put her in a house with lights
on a warm May evening. Place a jug of bluebells
in the hall. Let the kitchen smell of baking. Have her
count nine birthday candles for her younger son.
Make her remember the hour's contentment and calm.

                    For here comes the storm
that will tear the wall from the side of the world.
Here spins the elder son in his teenage despair,
lost in a darkness too difficult to steer, his hand
rising against himself as if it were a stranger.

Watch the father's attempts to bring him back,
breath after breath. Follow the sirens to the hospital's
fluorescence. Shrink from the ferocity of questions.
Feel the night tumble into disbelief. Imagine your own son,
sixteen years old, on that metal gurney. Recall the time
when it could have been you.

See the mother wake next morning (if she sleeps at all)
to a fog sticking to things like a white pall. Observe
the tenderness as she holds her younger son extra close,
the anguish as she looks her husband in the eye.
Hear them swear not to let this horror spread backwards
to taint all they knew, not to let bitterness enter.
But oh, the wild horses of the mind – fault, blame,
guilt, regret, shame, stigma – how hot their breath,
how keen they are to canter.

Consider how grief can drown the strongest faith,
how it takes months to learn to walk on water.
Consider the love and skill it needs to find a 'yes'
for all the 'no's', to unpick harrowing untruths
that claw at past and future.

But behold, here she is,
the same woman, years later, lighting candles
in a large room. See her open the door to mother
after mother. Smell the lilac, coffee, ginger.

Rise
Bethany Rivers

(for Michele)

When you fall down, fall down to your knees,
bent over double, on the bedroom floor,
the bed too far to crawl to,
sun, shadow, rain or snow
makes no difference to your splintering
stomach, the tsunami in your head,
what is it, tell me, what is it
that gets you on your feet again,
what is it that stops you going down
to the river with stones in your pockets?

I ask you this six months later, sitting
on a stool at your kitchen counter, as you percolate
coffee in the dim glow of your sanctuary. This is the
room you love most, brown walls, old signs
from the 1940s, crates nailed to the walls,
silver pans hanging in size order. I know
you've been there. I know you've got up
off the floor. Tell me.

What you say next offers no comfort at all.
Though you want to: your oil lamp isn't bright
enough to light the depths of my well.

I'm a single person, in the world, thirsty.
You're a single mother, with a thread
to the future. You have no choice.

Body Balance
Isabel Palmer

*For a friend, whose son hanged himself while she
was at a gym class.*

At the spinning class you say,
I don't want your Christmas card.
You leave only nameless days unbroken,
sweep birthdays, anniversaries
and Christmas into corners.

Everyone remembers
and forgets. Our talk is silk:
butterflies winding round
a violet woodland, afraid
to leave...and I can never

speak about my son who's
gone to war...Everyone
remembers where they were
when... Elvis, Diana,
the Twin Towers' falling man...

She was here, with me.
Shine your chest up.
His last breath.
Hug muscle into bones.
The night before, after they talked.

Feel your spine anchored
between floor and ceiling.
His Desert Island
music, still playing.
Look beyond your fingertips.

Not stretching, reaching
on a slow tide towards him;
the air, filled with mountains,
forests, seagulls far-off,
too thin to hold him.

A Boy Stands
Belinda Rimmer

A boy stands at the sea wall
on the Promenade des Anglais, Nice.
I, beside him, note his soft canvas shoes
and the way he stares over the edge.

On the Promenade des Anglais, Nice,
I read the sign in English: *Danger. No Jumping.*
By the way he stares over the edge,
it seems the boy has jumping on his mind.

I read the sign in English: *Danger. No Jumping.*
The boy's eyes flick away.
It seems he has jumping on his mind.
If only I had the language to ask.

The boy's eyes flick away
and rest on the rocks below.
If only I had the language to ask
what would I say: be brave, let life progress?

The boy's eyes rest on the rocks below
I, beside him, note his soft canvas shoes.
What would I say: be brave, let life progress?
A boy stands at the sea wall.

Son
Helen Kay

He loved optical illusion books.
Slowly bring the paper to your eyes.
The bird slides inside the cage.

Holiday snap. You wrapped him
in a Tweenies towel, a hot dog
with mustard hair and salty toes.

Mug shot. MISSING. His skull
is a worm can. You long for him
home, to put the lid back on.

You grip two photographs.
Slowly bring them to your eyes
to slide him into the towel again.

Inscription
claire e.potter

Here we three shared our grief,
shifted pine needles to plant petunias
at the tree's collar; the wind chime we'd hung
made thick air, hot between us, feel lighter.
But that storm, its gale force flood,
biblical, snatched the tree; we had nowhere
to go to remember you then. Did the roots
give up easily? And you?

We dispersed, too.

Long years on, I came back to where
there should have been a shady spot
with the memorial bench, your name to rest on,
a spider's web in that live oak, a bird in full song
but nothing
      —except a pond nearby, a heron
        that swooped into the sky. And the leaf I'd kept,

the leaf tangible in my hand has veins,
it's those veins; they make you vital still,
they double me over.

Sitting Under a Pine Tree
Zoe Piponides

I find comfort in the most expected of places
Like my bed when the sheets smell of sour cream
And there's space on the floor for just my feet,
Or when the shower head's flushing hot steam
And I'm handling a razor in the right direction.

I seek comfort in the most expected of places
Like the top shelf of the fridge or middle door
Below the hob, the glass cabinet above
The stereo and how it meets a yellow sofa,
trays, crumbs tucked away in cushions.

I seek comfort in the most expected of places
Like the shade under heaving branches,
A needle rug beneath bare toes, the crunch
And crackle as I wrap tobacco tails and trace
The scent of my own unwashed breath.

I find comfort in the most expected of places
Like the bottom drawer of my bedside table,
Thumbs popping foil, the crinkle as I extract
My so-called lozenges, my white-kite knights,
The gradual rising light, its entry points.

Ghost Wave
Michelle Diaz

You haven't gone, but your energy is skeletal.
No capacity for drama, you vacate slowly.
Your story won't make front page news.

This closing of blinds, handing yourself in,
will largely go unnoticed.
Rethink.
There is nobody here to rethink.

This is a clean protest, a way
to unlove yourself out of *this*.
Open a door into steady ivory.

This is a shut mouth,
a whisper for nothing.

A slow fall downwards.

face
Alan Girling

he found his friend
found the body of his friend
found the body kneeling
kneeling without a prayer

he found the body kneeling
kneeling at the end
of an invisible thread
of the finest gossamer
as though it had always been there

he found the body
saw the face
saw the skin chalk
the eyes glass
he found the body
searched the face
for a reflection in the glass
name on the tongue

he found the body
he found the body of his friend
he found his friend
and kneeling
without a prayer
he fell off the face
of love

Time To Check In
Salena Godden

The shop windows are
all orange and Halloween

The toothless plastic pumpkin
grins with a wicked flame

The days get grey
as wrung out ropes

Fire-yellow leaves
become a rotten mulch

Cold coffin toppings and
decay in the gutters

The stars expire and
here comes the dark

It's the beginning
Of suicide season

My friends feel it
we leave messages
to make sure we're all ok

"Can we meet for a quiet pint,
just us, and just the one, to catch up
and check in…"

I imagine a death watch beetle
tapping out its vigil to attract mates

Hey you Squirrel Nutkin
did you save enough nuts and seeds?
Will you make it through the long dark?

Last year's moth-balled winter coat looks hopeless,
but it's a good job it still fits over everything you're hiding.

Because here comes winter

Pensioners freeze in their beds
homeless people die in shop doorways
refugees drown in frozen seas
the poor will eat their young

The noisy get busy
packaging premature season's greetings
stocking up on mince pies and port
soaking fruit for the figgy pudding

Poor poets drown their sorrows
artists nail down the canvas sails and
musicians hide from bailiffs
we all burn your rejection letters for light

The mice come and get thin and hungry
And spiders, here come the spiders

The Colony closed down
the pubs close down
the libraries close down
the circus left town

And they tell us poetry don't sell
art is the first thing
on the fire.

Here comes the cold, so beware,
wary you don't get trapped
beneath ice,
again.

Just hold your breath
and get to Christmas

Just hold your breath
and make it to Easter

No...hang on!

You just have to
make it through January
and fucking death is January.

Then to February
fucking murder
is bloody Valentines

But I heart you!
I really do

And I don't want to lose you
like I lost the path
And I don't want to lose you
in the dark.

We don't mean to get lost -
but we don't always get what we want
or say what we mean.

Goodbye summer

You come down so hard
you go through the ceiling
it's all cobwebs and fog and soup

You've been having trouble breathing
grabbing space to breathe

It's like kicking and punching
under chunks of frozen time

A tired bee is trapped and
banging it's face against time's window

But I hope you can hear me writing this
I had no credit to hear your message
and you had no money to return my call

Oh my love
I remember this crash

It's that old orange moth eaten jumper
You push your thumbs through the sleeve

It is that time of letting go
We must make sure we hold on to each other
We must make sure

We meet for
just the one to
catch up
and check in...

Just the one to
catch up
and check in...

Just the one to
catch up
and check in...

Just the one.

Just an acquaintance
Alastair Hesp

You came to me in an instant,
crossing a brook,
you knew my epitaph,
before I knew of stillness.
I thought you might have spoken more
on how I wanted to open the door of a moving car,
or how each tall building invited me to the top floor.
You shook my hand
when I didn't offer it.
You touched my heart, but not on Valentines Day
when blood ceased to circulate.
I wanted to play,
even though you didn't have the time.
You had a schedule to keep.

Eleven Men
Joelle Taylor

Did the sea recognise your face   did you look like someone it
once knew   did your wings remember your hands   did the
sea open its legs for you   and through the wet gap   could
you see yourself as a child   that boy I loved   who spoke
over me all summer   the bad grammar of your face   curled
against thought   digging your pen into paper   as though
there were something   on the other side of the sheet   some
meat   just out of reach   did the sea reach for you   was the
sinking   was the cold   how hard the air   your parents
were the waves the fists of schoolchildren   beating you into a
different body?

Did you roll up your right trouser leg   was the last cycle part
of the same cycle did the oil stain look like my smile   did
you wear the wrong belt   was it too thick, too tongue   were
you trying to keep the words in   are you tourniquet, boy
are you autumn leaf   are you sudden night   the cold is
coming   did you see your shadow step away from your body
did you become part of the clock   pendulum boy   did you
tick   how can a boy tick without exploding   did your
shadow burst in to crows   did the crows carry your coffin
did they hum   the song of waiting?

Did the tracks below you seem like threads in a web   did you
become stuck   is that why we found you there   buzzing
what did the last face say to you   was she a crowd   did she
see you   how can a thousand people walk past   and not one
of them see you   did you eat yourself before jumping   are

you one of the thousand   were you there for years before we
found you   Vitruvian   neon   a flashing shop window?

What did the ground say when it met you   did it ask after your
mother   the kids   did it open for you   was it door   who was
waiting on the other side   in a room dressed like childhood
nodding like a relative   those teeth   that hair   was it you   are
you relative   will your children look like you   did death wear
your first face or the last?

Did you notice how like rosary white pills are   did you pray on
the swallowing   the chalk outline inside your skin   did you
make Saints of all those who did not love you   did you worship
at their ugly   and when the bottle was turned inside-out   was
it a pocket   and inside the pocket   was there a note   was it
folded like a sleeping man   and when wakened did the note say
something about their being   so many questions?

are you sure you are dead   then why are you sat beside me?

Lazarus
Mario Petrucci

There are things perhaps
a father should not write –
how his five-year-old clings
through night in fits of sleep

almost as a woman might
to the man lost in grief
stroking his face his feet
caressing him back to life.

And what if that Lazarus
whose absent wife brought
no tenderness to his tomb
who died alive awaiting

the lover's Pentecost
felt his doomed body visited
in stupor of emergent death
not by the man of the Cross

but by innocent son
by spotless daughter
who melt a stiffened heart
and stir the stifled breath?

Oiling Brakes
Anthony Anaxagorou

We are suffering seven directions at once – C.K. Williams

you say I shouldn't visit / wait for the meds to kick in /
how it's all ox bullocks knocking around a poacher's sack /

you say I sound happier / I listen to the ways you breathe /
a beanbag kicked around by drunks in June /

you ask if it's raining / I say the ocean holds four out of five
living things / you take another drag / exhale scaffolding

your voice snake skin / I ask if you need me to bring anything /
you say only the best bits / how everyone sleeps

trapped inside someone they can't stand /
how your mate made a rope by herself / for her neck

how nobody knew how / clever bastard / who was sick
of seeing herself drooling through therapy /

three thousand hooved feet rushing over a tunnel /
a voice calling for you to finish / you say quick /

give me one more to think about / I say more than half
the British public believe in life after death

inhaling crows / you wait before saying /
what a bunch of nutters / why bother with facts

how our conversation's recorded / the voice again
calling / only this time you're gone.

The picture I keep of you has aged / us oiling brakes / you
peddling up a hill / storming down / palms to the sky

needing nothing / saying when a body drowns / water
compresses gasses in the chest / exploding the heart

who told you that / and you laugh / holding my head
under water / blood thumping against its first symptom /

the cry of a young bird on the bank / fallen from its nest /
you / lifting its suffering up to your mouth like a tonic /

its body secular / slower than a wound in a painting / go on /
name it / but I couldn't / you / hurling it far into the brambles /

racing up the next hill / a puncture / before the fall
breaks / screeching / at the foot of my ears / to stop.

Seven Senryu in Memory of Brian Karr Harter (1969-1987)
Carrie Etter

stepping up to the casket my noisy heartbeat

my reflection huge in the funeral parlor mirror

nearing his gravestone
the letters begin to blur--
January fog

remembering his suicide
winter hardens
the soil

visiting the graves
my legs sink
in deepening snow

remembering his suicide--
    stepping slowly
    across the moonlit bridge

remembering his suicide all these acorns

Rosemary
Janet Smith

When you came I dressed you
      in autumn leaves, their crumpled mustiness
      fitted your small bones

I swaddled you with feathers from the magpies
      that visited the garden
      their colours like your hair,
all the world's rainbows

I picked garlic from the corners
      of the bitter November soil
      hung them on strings of sun-shredded
burnet, strong and pliable to protect you

I washed carefully the fox's discarded
      fur, wove it with the crow's
    wings and the shells I had collected

I picked rose madder
      made a mordant of vinegar
      sewed the hues of the autumn
hedgerow into your vest

    when the robin came she gave
me a red feather, a blessing
    a bright eye to watch over you
a bobbin of thread to entertain you

I showed you the April wild-green
when the gold crests came
the throstle and the blue tit

the jay, and the bullfinch paired
    like the blackbird, rarely apart
picking through last year's raspberry canes
greeting old friends with a tsct tsch

You held a fledgling
blackbird too sudden from its nest,
its warm heart beat soothed your fingers
your tears for its short life
its soft weight
lay cradled in
your small hands.

Bath time memories
Janet Jenkins

Every one of these bubbles is one of our memories,
I'm going to collect them all up in this sponge to keep them safe.
I miss you and I know you still remember me.
You had to go away because you were sad,
but I'm happy you were my daddy and every time I see bubbles,
I remember the fun times we had blowing and bursting them,
while laughing and splashing each other.

An Improper Kindness
Christina Thatcher

Leave rehab. Come sit on my knee
like you did when you were my
much littler brother so I can tell you

of a place where the bricks of our childhood
home still stand, the kitchen smelling sweet
of pumpkin pie and whipped cream.

Our first pups and geese gather there,
it takes away the pain in teeth and brain,
stays blue-skied and cloudless.

When someone speaks it makes sense
and they smile: nothing is confusing.
Everyone is kind and there are no expectations.
You don't have to be a man.

I know I shouldn't be telling you now,
should only speak of this place
when you're old and rightfully dying.
Now, I should say:

you must solider on, start again
with new medicine, new job, new girl,
new family, new home.

But you are so tired and the light
of the halcyon place is getting brighter
and warmer, coming just into reach,
and so I tell you to go, open the door:

be happy.

The Ekphrasis of Self-annihilation
Asim Khan

there is a bind to observation. consider me
observing you. speaking out the language of dreams;

an ambiguous voice. particles in space, periods of time
unfolding. that you were my dark thought that for years

i believed i had harvested. that now, i come to see
as a plague of images that seemed like screams

in my mind. this considered destruction of self;
reflective. though it lingers, it emerges poetic,

in an instant, like here. of captured light, and darkness.
if i leave, what part chooses to stay?

A Single Atom in an Ion Trap
Glyn Edwards

A single atom in an ion trap
headlines a clipped page left
on a staffroom table above a
photograph of a pale blue dot
trapped between electrodes
barely two millimetres apart
suspended in an electric field
in a quiet Oxford laboratory
to create a direct and visceral bridge
between the quantum world
and macroscopic reality in the
frame of a digital camera held
at a vacuum chamber window
as blue-violet lasers illuminate
a strontium atom absorbing
and emitting their pale light
becoming visible to the eye

for weeks after they buried you
I picked blueschist off my shoes
rubbed it away from my fingers
never saw you crossing the yard
heard coughing from your room
noticed names change on doors
on the front of children's books
never thought death could be a
to any creation as divine as here
or that on a shelf quarried into
some silent strip of our universe
your omnipotence could form
again and find a way to share
a space with someone always
alone in an empty staffroom
finding blue flecks on floor tiles
sitting beside your empty seat

what might live on the other side of the moon
Martin Hayes

Jamie has started working harder than usual
he has started coming in for work 20 minutes early
making a big noise about cleaning down his work station
so that everyone can see and hear
that Jamie is coming in for work 20 minutes early

he is now making sure that his fleet attendance forms
are filled in by the 11 o'clock deadline
when before they used to lay around his desk
with crumbs from bacon sandwiches and coffee cup rings all
        over them

he is actually talking to customers and colleagues now
engaging and witty and sympathetic
looking people in the eye and smiling
when before he used to hide away from everything
swerve any intimacy or confrontation
getting up to go into the toilet whenever he sensed a
        'situation' developing

his fingers float along his keyboard now
when before they used to just about manage to rise
before dropping down like wrecking balls onto those keys
his eyes and his demeanor and his breathing
everything about him is lighter now
more in sync
as he tells us across the table
that he's met a new girl with flaming red hair and a tounge

that licks up life from the sky and can hold stars in the back
        of her throat
who reads literature out to him after they've had sex
who is a vegan and who has got him eating lentils and fruit
lots and lots of fruit
who he holds hands with on walks through the park
talking about the birds and the sea which before
he thought must live on the other side of the moon
never once about work
or the supervisors or the couriers
who used to drive him into corners
who used to hammer him into the floor
who used to make him feel constantly trapped
as he finishes off his 4th apple
adding as he gets up to go back into work
that also
he hasn't once thought about killing himself
in a whole month.

hold me warm blooded thing
Shaun Hill

in this midst of this *i love you sometimes*
we were pleading the way the dying do:

> hold me warm blooded thing.

> hold me like the other men
> who are not silent round a coffin.

lips, blue as frozen strawberries soon
we are bleeding the way the living do:

> hold me warm blooded thing.

> hold me as if touch exists,
> as if it isn't just another myth.

i put your fingers in my mouth the way
i think i'm supposed to, so why don't you

> hold me warm blooded thing?

> hold me how a body does a name,
> how a pin holds down a grenade.

yes, we're a magnet for disaster the way
the earth is at its poles but i need you to

> hold me warm blooded thing.

> hold me until i'm nothing but
> weeping, until i'm nothing but

> water & salt.

In Which I Compose the Note but Then Talk Myself into Living

Gram Joel Davies

Finding these words, you already know that
you will carry on, forming pictures in overexposed shots,
not losing hope that some aspect of self persists.
Never call a loved one selfish for passing through earth
to where a man alone may feed the knots of trees.
An old razor has drawn a doorway through a membrane,
has whittled away the edge of experience to a thinness
of bad choices. I have gone. Hairy with failure, until its beard,
as darkness, defines identity. Remember, but have awareness,
kindness will draw you to suppose what it is like
when wrists part lips to speak with an arterial shh;
to confront the resinous half-hours which feel unbearable
to me. You are blameless. Find reason to go on.

To me: you are blameless, find reason to go on,
to confront the resinous half-hours which feel unbearable,
when wrists part lips to speak with an arterial shh.
Kindness will draw you to suppose what it is like
as darkness defines identity, remember. But have awareness
of bad choices. I have gone hairy with failure, until its beard
has whittled away the edge of experience to a thinness,
an old razor; has drawn a doorway through a membrane
to where a man, alone, may feed. The knots of trees
never call a loved one selfish. For, passing through Earth,
not losing hope that some aspect of self persists,
you will carry on, forming pictures in overexposed shots.
Finding these words, you already know that.

Evening Prayer
Abi Budgen

Evening hangs in pastel hues
Iridescent, sweet and warm
Holding its breath
Dogs and bikes and ordinary things
Pass it by

Day, relentless
Parched and gasping
Now quenched with calm
Breathes out slowly
Releases all tension

Another spirit
Home

A Dream
David Calcutt

You were on the river, heading away downstream,
your powerful shoulders working the paddle –
dip, pull, lift, dip, pull – each stroke a perfect slice
through the black water, that gathered and ruckled
about the blade – lift, dip, pull –

as in the time we were on the river together,
that autumn morning of mist drifting up through
the highbanked trees and the fine rain that soaked
our clothes and skin and hair and made us happy.
A good time. The two of us together on the river.

Now you were alone and it was night.
I was leaning on the windowsill, looking out
and if you had turned you would have seen me there,
a ghost face at the glass haunting your leaving.
You did not look back. All your concentration

strained towards the journey you were making
and I was powerless to stop you, just as I was powerless
to turn away from watching. No call of mine
would bring you back. For payment, the river
had taken my voice, and I was forbidden to enter

where you were going.

Listen to this
Stewart Carswell

The river is fed by streams that pour
sound down the hillside. A season of rain
fattens it. The level has risen
higher than I expected, but it is level still

and *that* is important: to stay balanced
no matter how much rain
has fallen, no matter how much you want
to flow with that water away from this place.

OUR CONTRIBUTORS (THANK-YOU!)

Anthony Anaxagorou is a British-born Cypriot award-winning poet, fiction writer, essayist, publisher and poetry educator. He has published nine volumes of poetry, a spoken-word EP and a collection of short stories. He has won multiple awards, most recently being shortlisted for the Jerwood Compton Poetry Fellowship. He is founder of Out-Spoken, spoken word night and press.

Romalyn Ante grew up in the Philippines and moved to the UK in 2005. She is the winner of Poetry London Clore Prize 2018 and joint-winner of the Manchester Writing Competition 2017. She also received Platinum Poetry Award from Creative Future Literary Award 2017, and her debut pamphlet, *Rice & Rain* (V.Press), received the 2018 Saboteur Award for Best Poetry Pamphlet.

Casey Bailey is a writer, poet, spoken word performer, rapper and secondary school senior leader, born and raised in Nechells, Birmingham. Casey released the short poetry collection *Waiting At Bloomsbury Park* with Big White Shed in 2017, and his debut full collection *Adjusted* with Verve Poetry Press. He finished in the top 4 of the BBC Edinburgh Fringe Slam 2018.

Abi Budgen is a musician, illustrator and until recently, a closet poet. Her poem *Evening Prayer* is dedicated to the loving memory of Val Long and Chris Long.

Lewis Buxton is a poet & and arts producer. In 2018, Lewis was the recipient of the 2018 UEA Literary Festival Bursary for Creative Writing and he won The Poetry School & Nine Arches Press, Primers Competition Volume Four. He has performed across the country and teaches creative writing. His first pamphlet *Weight* is forthcoming. He currently lives in Norwich.

David Calcutt is a playwright, poet and novelist. He has written original plays and adaptations for theatre and BBC radio, and a number of his theatre scripts are published by Oxford University Press. He has written four collections of poetry, the latest being *The Last of the Light is not the Last of the Light,* published by Fair Acre Press, and four novels, published by Ocford and Barefoot Books. He is Associate Artist with Midlands

Actors Theatre and company writer for Regional Voice Theatre.

Louisa Campbell has been both psychiatric nurse and patient, and now turns these experiences into poems. She has two pamphlets published: *The Happy Bus,* (2017, Picaroon Poetry), and *The Ward,* (2018, Paper Swans Press). She lives in Kent.

Diana Cant is a child psychotherapist and poet, who has spent all her professional life working with young people in various sorts of distress. One of the aims of her poetry is to give these young people a voice that is seldom heard. She lives and works in Kent, and has been published in various anthologies and journals.

Gary Carr has been involved with poetry for more than twenty years and has had more than fifty poems published in anthologies and literary magazines including Voices of 1919, Under the Radar and The Interpreter's House. He runs Spoken Worlds open mic night and Runaway Writers' Group in Burton-on-Trent. More of his poetry can be seen at gary-carr.me.uk.

Stewart Carswell is from the Forest of Dean, and currently lives in Cambridgeshire. He studied Physics at Southampton University, and has a PhD from the University of Bristol. His poems have recently been published in Envoi, The Poetry Shed, and Ink Sweat & Tears. His debut pamphlet is *Knots and branches* (Eyewear, 2016). http://stewartcarswell. wordpress.com Twitter: @stewcarswell

Gram Joel Davies lives in Devon. His debut *Bolt Down This Earth* (V. Press 2017) was described by The Poetry Book Society as "a striking collection, full of vitality and enjoyment of the poetic craft." His poetry has lately been published in Poetry Wales, Until the Stars Burn Out and as weekly poem at Oxford Brookes Poetry Centre. Find him online at https://gramjoeldavies.uk

Michelle Diaz has been widely published in both print and online. She won the 2018 Christabel Hopesmith NHS Poetry Competition. She lives in the strange town of Glastonbury with her son who has Tourette Syndrome. Her debut pamphlet *The Dancing Boy* is due out in February 2019 with Against the Grain Press.

Glyn Edwards has been a Guest Editor of The Lonely Crowd and will publish his first collection of poetry with The Lonely Press in early 2018. He is a trustee of The Terry Hetherington Prize and is co-editor of the Partian-published Cheval Anthology. He is a MA pupil at MMU and teaches in North Wales.

American expatriate **Carrie Etter** has published four collections of poetry, most recently *The Weather in Normal* (UK: Seren, US: Station Hill, 2018), a Poetry Book Society Recommendation. She is a Reader in Creative Writing at Bath Spa University.

RM Francis is author of three chapbooks, *Transitions* (Black Light Engine Room, 2015), *Orpheus* (Lapwing Publications, 2016) and *Corvus' Burnt-Wing Love Balm and Cure-All* (Black Light Engine Room, 2018). He completed his PhD at the University of Wolverhampton. Original Plus are publishing his fourth pamphlet in 2019. His full collection is due in 2020 with Smokestack Books.

Alam Girling writes poetry, sometimes fiction, plays, etc. in Richmond, British Columbia, He has been published in such venues as Panoply, Blue Skies, FreeFall, Hobart, SmokeLong Quarterly and The MacGuffin. His work has placed in three poetry contests, been displayed in shop windows and read or heard by hundreds.

Salena Godden is author of poetry collections *Under The Pier* (Nasty Little Press) and *Fishing in the Aftermath: Poems 1994-2014* (Burning Eye); literary childhood memoir *Springfield Road* (Ubound) and *Shade* published in the award-winning anthology *The Good Immigrant* (Unbound). Her live poetry album *LIVEwire* was released in 2017 with indie spoken word label Nymphs and Thugs and was shortlisted for the Ted Hughes Award. *Pessimism Is For Lightweights* - 13 pieces of courage and resistance' was published in the summer of 2018 by Rough Trade Books. The title poem *Pessimism is for Lightweights* is currently a pubic poetry art piece displayed at the Arnolfini Gallery, Bristol. A BBC documentary following 12 months of her latest work-in-progress *Mrs Death Misses Death* was broadcast in December 2018 - This will be a debut fiction with soundtrack, exploring Death as a woman and themes of life and death, loss and love.

Emily Harrison is a young short fiction and poetry writer from North Yorkshire, Emily has recently discovered that she actually likes writing, despite everything she may have previously said. She can be found procrastinating on Twitter @emily__harrison. *sadness is a room* is her third poem to go to print, and the most personal poem she has penned to date.

John Hawkhead is a writer and illustrator from the South West of England. His book of haiku and senryu *Small Shadows* is available from Alba Publishing. His twitter account is @HawkheadJohn.

Martin Hayes was born and has lived around the Edgware Road area of London all of his life. He has worked in the courier industry for over 30 years and is the author of four books of poetry: *Letting Loose The Hounds*, (Redbeck Press, 2001). *When We Were Almost Like Men*, (Smokestack, 2015). *The Things Our Hands Once Stood For*, (Culture Matters, 2018) and *Roar!* (Smokestack, 2018).

Alastair Hesp is a poet from Yorkshire, England. He was recently shortlisted for the Indigo Dreams first-pamphlet award and his poetry has appeared in literary journals such as The Canons Mouth and The French Literary Review. His poetry concerns a tense, paradoxical, violent love of a life in common.

Shaun Hill is a Nine Arches Press mentee, and will exhibiting at UK Young Artists City Takeover 2019. His work has also been anthologised in *Play: Poems and Pictures* (PaperDart Press).

Paul Howarth is a poet, a photographer and a librarian. He was born in Chester and now lives near the Suffolk coast with his wife and two boys. He has poetry published in various magazines and anthologies, including Under the Radar, The Fenland Reed, The Emma Press Anthology of the Sea and The Emma Press Anthology of Love.

Rosie Jackson is a poet and workshop leader who lives near Frome, Somerset. *What the Ground Holds* (Poetry Salzburg, 2014) was followed in 2016 by *The Light Box* (Cultured Llama) and *The Glass Mother: A Memoir* (Unthank). She won 1st prize in the Stanley Spencer competition 2017; 1st at Wells and 2nd in Frogmore Papers and Torbay, 2018. www.rosiejackson.org.uk

Janet Jenkins lives in Staffordshire. She is the leader of The Lichfield Poets and takes part in the group's performances at festivals and other events. She also reads at open mics throughout The Midlands. Her poems have been included in a number of literary magazines and anthologies, the latest being *Diversifly: Poetry and Art on Britain's Urban Birds* (Fairacre Press. 2018)

Helen Kay is based near Crewe Helen and is doing a part-time MA in Poetry at MMU. Her poems have appeared in various magazines including Interpreter's House, Stand and Rialto. Prizes include runner up in Cheshire Prize for Literature and 2nd in the Leeds Poetry Peace Prize (2018). She co-ordinates a project called Dyslexia, Poetry and Imagination (on facebook).

Asim Khan lives and works in Birmingham/Coventry, where he is also a PhD student as part of the Warwick Writing Programme. His poetry has appeared and is forthcoming in various online and print publications; www.asimk.uk @ecopoetic

Charles Lauder Jr was born and raised in Texas and has lived in the UK for several years. He has published two pamphlets, *Bleeds* and *Camouflaged Beasts*. His debut poetry collection, *The Aesthetics of Breath*, will be published in late 2019 by V. Press.

Hannah Linden has won or been placed in competitions and is published widely, most recently with Magma, Lighthouse, The Interpreter's House, Under the Radar and the Humanagerie anthology; as well as on several online webzines. She is working towards her first collection, *Wolf Daughter*, which will explore the impact of parental suicide. She was 12 when her father died by suicide. Twitter: @hannahl1n

Jane Lovell has been widely published in journals and anthologies. She has won the Flambard Prize and been shortlisted for several awards including the Basil Bunting Prize, the Robert Graves Prize and the Periplum Book Award. Her most recent publication is *Metastatic* from Against the Grain Poetry Press. Jane won this year's Coast to Coast to Coast Portfolio Prize, the Wealden Literary Festival Writing Prize, the Terrain.org Poetry Contest and the Wigtown Poetry Prize.

Nick Makoha's debut collection *Kingdom of Gravity* was shortlisted for the 2017 Felix Dennis Prize for Best First Collection and nominated by The Guardian as one of the best books of 2017. He is a Cave Canem

Graduate Fellow and Complete Works Alumni. Learn more about his many accomplishments at www.nickmakoha.com

Liam McCormick is a writer from Glasgow and The Black Isle. He has been on the BBC, radio and TV, and performs across the country. His latest work *BEAST* was longlisted for the 2018 Scottish Mental Health Association Edinburgh Fringe Award. He would describe his work as funnier than you'd think. *BEAST* is available to buy from Burning Eye Books.

Andrew McMillan's books are the multi-award winning *physical* and, most recently, *playtime*, a PBS recommendation for Autumn 2018 and a Sunday Times Poetry Book of the Year. He is Senior Lecturer in the Manchester Writing School at MMU.

Abegail Morley was named as one of the five British poets to watch in 2017 – Huffington Post. Her debut, *How to Pour Madness into a Teacup*, was shortlisted for the Forward Prize Best First Collection. *Cutting the Cord* is forthcoming from Nine Arches Press. She is one of the co-editors at Against the Grain Press, an innovative small independent poetry publisher .

Katrina Naomi's Japanese-themed pamphlet *Typhoon Etiquette* will be published by Verve Poetry Press in April 2019. She was awarded an Authors' Foundation grant from the Society of Authors for work on her third full poetry collection to be published by Seren in June 2020. Her most recent collection is *The Way the Crocodile Taught Me* (Seren, 2016) www.katrinanaomi.co.uk.

Antony Owen is from Coventry and is the author of five collections of poetry often focused upon modern issues of conflict. His latest collection, *The Nagasaki Elder* (V.Press) was shortlisted for The Hughes Award for new work in poetry (2017). His next collection is out in 2019 with KF&S Press.

Isabel Palmer is co-editor of Flarestack Poets. *Ground Signs* was a PBS Pamphlet Choice. Her first full collection was *Atmospherics* with a foreword by Andrew Motion, in 'Home Front' (Bloodaxe). She won the National Army Poetry Competition 2018 and took third prize in the Robert Graves Poetry Competition. As Poet-in-Residence at the National Army Museum, she ran workshops for Chelsea Pensioners..

Ian Patterson has had poems featured in South Bank Poetry, Magma, Strix, DogEar, and has been shortlisted a number of times by the Bridport Prize. He works and lives in Suffolk and is a frequent visitor to London.

Award-winning UK poet, ecologist and PhD physicist **Mario Petrucci** has held major poetry residencies at the Imperial War Museum and with BBC Radio 3. *Heavy Water: a poem for Chernobyl* (Enitharmon, 2004) secured the Daily Telegraph/ Arvon Prize. *i tulips* (Enitharmon, 2010) exemplifies Petrucci's distinctive combination of innovation and humanity. www.mariopetrucci.com

Zoe Piponedes currently teaches English in Cyprus. Her writing has been commended and shortlisted in the UK, including the following competitions: Alan Sillitoe, Ink Pellet/Poetry Review, National Academy of Writing: Countries of the Mind, Word Hut Short Story. Her poems have appeared in various publications, including CALM, The Font, The Pickled Body and The Huffington Post.

clare e.potter is a bilingual poet/performer currently directing a documentary. Produced Arts Council funded poetry/jazz collaboration about Hurricane Katrina. Poetry residencies include the Landmark Trust, Moravian School, Pennsylvania. John Tripp Award for Spoken Poetry winner, second book forthcoming, funded by Literature Wales bursary. A Hay Festival Writer at Work, widely published in Welsh/ English. www.clareawenydd.com

Peter Raynard is editor of Proletarian Poetry: poems of working class lives (www.proletarianpoetry.com). He is the author of two books of poetry; his debut collection *Precarious* (Smokestack Books, 2018) and *The Combination: a poetic coupling of the Communist Manifesto* (Culture Matters, 2018) @proletarianpoet

Brenda Read-Brown has won many poetry slams and performed all over the UK and abroad, and written several prize-winning plays. Her first poetry collection *Arbitrary edges*, was published in 2013, and the second, Like love, was published by V press in 2018.

Victoria Richards is a journalist and writer. In 2017/18 she was short-listed in the Bath Novel Award and the Lucy Cavendish College Fiction Prize, was highly commended for poetry in the Bridport Prize and came third in The London Magazine Short Story Competition. She is one of three winning poets for Primers: Volume Four, with Nine Arches Press. Find her at www.twitter.com/nakedvix or www.victoriarichards.co.uk.

Belinda Rimmer has worked as a psychiatric nurse, lecturer and creative arts practitioner. Her poems are in magazines, on-line journals and anthologies. In 2017, she won the Poetry in Motion Competition to turn her poem into a film, shown Internationally. She came second in the 2018 Ambit Poetry Competition. Her first poetry pamphlet will be published next year by Indigo Dreams.

Bethany Rivers' debut pamphlet, *Off the wall,* was published by Indigo Dreams. Her second collection is due out in the summer: *the sea refuses no river,* from Fly on the Wall press. *Tell it slant: a writer's guide,* is due out in spring from Victorina Press. She is editor of 'As Above So Below', an online spiritual poetry magazine. She runs writing courses and mentors the writing of novels, memoir, children's stories and poetry. www.writingyourvoice.org.uk

Stephen Seabridge is the first Poet Laureate of Stoke-on-Trent in Staffordshire. He enjoys writing about aspects of male identity, the regional, and the surprising confluences poetry has a habit of unearthing. His work is available online and in print. He is humbled to be part of this varied, powerful anthology.

Richard Skinner's poetry first appeared in the Faber anthology *First Pressings* (1998) and since then in anthologies for William Blake, John Berger and Médicines Sans Frontières. He has published three books of poems with Smokestack: *the light user scheme* (2013), *Terrace* (2015) & *The Malvern Aviator* (2018).available online and in print.

Caroline Smith lives in Wembley where she works as the immigration and asylum caseworker for a London MP. Although originally trained as a sculptor, Caroline has now published three books of poetry. Her most recent, *The Immigration Handbook,* published by Seren Books was shortlisted for the Ted Hughes Award 2016.

Janet Smith is a Scientist and writer based in Birmingham. She has published poetry in Abridged, Orbis, South, Under the Radar and others. In "Tour de Vers" (Red Squirrel Press), and in anthologies by Offa's Press, Flarestack Poets. A prizewinner in Hippocrates prize, "write-a-Bridge", others.

Joelle Taylor is an award-winning poet, playwright and author who recently toured Europe, Australia and South East Asia with her latest collection *Songs My Enemy Taught Me*. She is the author of 3 full poetry collections and is completing her debut book of short stories, *The Night Alphabet*. She founded SLAMbassadors, the UK's national youth slam championships, for the Poetry Society.

MT Taylor's poem has its basis in true events and so the subject of this project is of personal concern. Her work has appeared in Northwords Now, The Glasgow Review of Books, Ink Sweat and Tears, The Lake, Algebra of Owls, and in The Interpreter's House. She has four children who still talk to her, and she still interrupts.

Christina Thatcher is a Creative Writing Lecturer at Cardiff Metropolitan University. Her poetry has featured in over 40 magazines and anthologies. Her debut collection, *More than you were*, was shortlisted for Bare Fiction's Debut Poetry Collection Competition in 2015 and was published by Parthian Books in 2017. To learn more please visit christinathatcher.com or follow her @writetoempower.

ABOUT THE POEMS

Oiling Brakes by Anthony Anaxagorou is from his forthcoming collection to be published by Penned In The Margins in Autumn 2019.

Multiple Choice **by Casey Bailey is from his Verve Poetry Press debut full collection** *Adjusted* **(Apr 18).**

Helen Calcutt's poem *Now my brother has died* appeared previously on Atrium Poetry.

The senryu of Carrie Etter's *Seven Senryu in Memory of Brian Karr Harter (1969-1987)* originally appeared individually in black bough, Blithe Spirit, Frogpond, Haiku Quarterly, and Presence.

Book Of The Dead by Nick Makoha is from his debut collection *Kingdom Of Gravity* (2017, Peeple Tree Press).

Caroline Smith's poem *Red Road Flats* first appeared in her Seren Collection *The Immigration Handvook* (2016).

All other poems in this book are previously unpublished.

HELEN THANKS...

Stuart Bartholomew at Verve Poetry Press, for opening the door and making this all possible, for your support, friendship, positivity, and guidance above and beyond; to my father David Calcutt for your creative input, strength, and editorial insights, and my mother Susan Calcutt for your endless inspiration and moral support.

To Deborah Alma for leading the way on anthologies with a cause; to Mario Petrucci for your wisdom and unmatched understanding of my creative vision; to Carolyn Jess-Cooke, who (without knowing it) formed my initial approach to gathering and ordering the poems. To Arifa Akbar for openly supporting this project; to Christina Thatcher who, as both a poet and a dear friend, guided me through my grief, and encouraged me to be creative with it. To Neil Wood and Fae Evelyn from CALM who initially gave the nod to this project and have been supportive ever since; to Adam Patel, for your patience, good humour, and sterling efforts in bridging communications between me and your design team; to Scott Silvey for your wonderful book design; to Peter Raynard for your exceptional copy editing skills; to every writer who submitted their work to this anthology, it was humbling to receive so many genuine works of the souls and spirit; to Jacques Lusseyran, whose book, 'And then there was light' offered quiet repose in moments of mild, editorial desperation.

To my partner, whose openness to this idea from the start gave me the strength to see it through. To my beautiful daughter, who sat at my feet and sang while I worked. To my brother, Jon Calcutt, whose strength of character and willpower is a testament to both male vigour and vulnerability. To my sister-in-law Aurelie Blondeau-Calcutt, for simply being beautiful and uplifting. To my nephew Tom, my dinosaur hero. To my extended family, Anna Price (oldest friend and ever-understanding sister) Joe Price, Paul Russell, Glenys Russell, Andrew Russell and Marian Russell, for your sincerity and courage. To Oliver Calcutt, for being the bravest little man I know. To Matthew Calcutt, for continuing to give, even after you thought you had nothing left. I love you.

www.vervepoetrypress.com
@VervePoetryPres
mail@vervepoetrypress.com